Bond

10 Minute Tests

8-9 years

Frances Down

Verbal Reasoning

Test 1: Sorting Words 1

Test time: 0 — 5 — 10 minutes

Underline the pair of words most similar in meaning.

Example: come, go   <u>roam, wander</u>   fear, fare

1 book, word   story, tale   letter, pen   5 stop, go   finish, halt   begin, end
2 sight, vision   expect, delay   common, unusual
3 caught, loose   criminal, prison   free, release
4 cheese, biscuits   dish, bowl   bread, jam

Underline the word in the brackets closest in meaning to the word in capitals.

Example: UNHAPPY   (unkind   death   laughter   <u>sad</u>   friendly)

6 TIMID   (nervous   bold   quick   expensive   brave)
7 MAIN   (water   chief   stay   part   pony)
8 UNDER   (over   beside   beneath   inside   outside)
9 VARIABLE   (plain   constant coloured   changeable fixed)
10 SINGE   (tuneful   carol   warm   beat   burn)
11 LIE   (down   sleep   bed   fib   truth)
12 CATCH   (escape   throw   capture   chase   ball)
13 WOMAN   (child   male   daughter   lady   man)
14 COMBINE   (harvest   divide   blend   separate   keep)
15 CHARGE   (attack   money   change   guard   coin)

Total

Test 2: Selecting Words 1

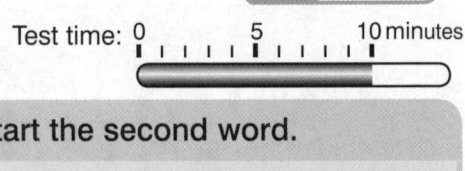

Test time: 0 — 5 — 10 minutes

Find the letter which will end the first word and start the second word.

Example: peac (_h_) ome

1 wis (__) ome   6 zer (__) nly   11 pal (__) ach
2 tin (__) olk   7 sic (__) ilt   12 lam (__) ook
3 com (__) ike   8 toy (__) pin   13 hal (__) ish
4 war (__) ess   9 shi (__) air   14 jaz (__) one
5 fle (__) rmy   10 fou (__) oar   15 car (__) cho

Total

TEST 3: Sorting and Selecting Words

Test time: 0 — 5 — 10 minutes

Underline the pair of words most opposite in meaning.

Example: cup, mug   coffee, milk   <u>hot, cold</u>

1	late, early	tea, breakfast	spare, extra
2	black, blue	scene, view	little, large
3	away, out	pencil, case	break, mend
4	below, above	in, on	top, upper
5	blue, bottle	calm, rough	hand, foot

Underline the pair of words most similar in meaning.

Example: come, go   <u>roam, wander</u>   fear, fare

6	improve, better	likely, doubtful	find, search
7	middle, end	attempt, try	pass, stop
8	stay, remain	fast, slow	healthy, unwell
9	rough, smooth	flood, drought	hard, difficult
10	honour, obey	rapid, slow	hurl, fling

Remove one letter from the word in capitals to leave a new word. The meaning of the new word is given in the clue.

Example: AUNT   an insect   ___ant___

11	WIND	come first	_____
12	HEATH	warmth	_____
13	CRANE	a walking stick	_____
14	BLEACH	seashore	_____
15	FLIGHT	not heavy	_____

3

Total

TEST 4: **Selecting Words 2**

Test time: 0 — 5 — 10 minutes

Underline two words, one from each group, that go together to form a new word. The word in the first group always comes first.

Example: (hand, <u>green</u>, for)   (light, <u>house</u>, sure)

1   (fore, hand, right)   (head, fit, sore)   5   (way, up, stand)   (ran, set, in)

2   (off, chatter, back)   (climb, box, on)   6   (fast, dog, car)   (pet, run, road)

3   (best, high, kind)   (light, friend, nest)   7   (time, clap, fish)   (wish, ping, rung)

4   (sock, wait, mush)   (or, foot, room)

Complete the following sentences by selecting the most sensible word from each group of words given in the brackets. Underline the words selected.

Example: The (<u>children</u>, books, foxes) carried the (houses, <u>books</u>, steps) home from the (greengrocer, <u>library</u>, factory).

8   Every (hair, night, holiday) before you go to (bed, London, school) you must brush your (dogs, teeth, cars).

9   Danielle's (coat, hill, garden) is (blue, wet, steep) with (red, winding, frightened) buttons.

10 The (frightened, hungry, loud) (dog, girl, balloon) gnawed on his (thumb, bone, firework).

11 The (pretty, clean, rusty) hinge on the garden (flower, gate, post) (squeaked, spoke, cycled) loudly.

12 Yesterday it (shone, rained, flew) heavily and there were (tall, deep, sunny) puddles all over the (sky, playground, pond).

13 The (rocket, train, promise) blasted into the (sky, rails, room) from the space (station, town, letter).

14 My (uncle, aunt, dog) Brian is my (pet's, mother's, desk's) (chair, brother, wall).

15 Mrs Briggs bent (up, down, along) to smell the (fragrant, cold, easy) rose in her (garden, bathroom, cupboard).

Total

Test 5: Anagrams 1

Rearrange the muddled letters in capitals to make a proper word. The answer will complete the sentence sensibly.

Example: A BEZAR is an animal with stripes. __ZEBRA__

1. On November 5th, we are going to a IEOKRWFR display. _____
2. Last Saturday and DYANUS, it rained all day. _____
3. Over the summer, our lawn needed constant WMNIOG. _____
4. Please be TUQEI and finish your work. _____
5. Samantha painted a beautiful CTPIREU. _____

Look at the first group of three words. The word in the middle has been made from the other two words. Complete the second group of three words in the same way, making a new word in the middle.

	Example:	PA**IN**	**IN**TO	**TO**OK	ALSO	__SOON__	ONLY
6		BUSH	SHOP	OPEN	RUST	_____	IRON
7		CARS	CAPE	RIPE	PARK	_____	LESS
8		HORN	HOLE	LEAP	MOON	_____	REAL
9		CHIP	CAKE	WAKE	FLAN	_____	HIRE
10		FAME	MESS	PASS	WAIT	_____	STEM
11		BITE	TEND	BOND	WIRE	_____	NEST
12		CURL	CUTE	TEAM	FORM	_____	ALSO
13		RISE	SEEN	ENDS	LIVE	_____	STIR
14		FLAG	FLAT	WHAT	PLUG	_____	THAN
15		STAG	SINK	WINK	KERB	_____	MISS

TEST 6: Anagrams 2

A B C D E F G H I J K L M N O P Q R S T U V W X Y Z

If these words were placed in alphabetical order, which word would come first? Underline the correct answer. The alphabet has been written out to help you.

1	brown	yellow	orange	white	purple
2	thigh	foot	chest	head	shoulder
3	July	August	September	October	November
4	trousers	triumph	trample	transport	tricky
5	product	profess	produce	profit	progress

In each line, underline the word which has its letters in alphabetical order.

6	petal	abbot	crime	tusks
7	salad	eight	flips	bossy
8	ghost	witch	moist	mouse
9	always	glory	stray	hover
10	itch	lost	bath	pole

Underline the word in each line which uses only letters from the first six letters of the alphabet.

11	baked	after	gladly	added
12	fable	guide	faced	caged
13	bead	ache	cats	fish
14	fill	dark	belt	cafe
15	card	fate	deaf	cake

TEST 7: Anagrams 3

Find the three-letter word which can be added to the letters in capitals to make a new word. The new word will complete the sentence sensibly.

Example: The cat sprang onto the MO. _____USE_____

1. The little boy cried when his BOON popped.
2. Neil likes bright colours like red and OGE.
3. Our hockey M is unbeaten so far this season.
4. Their GAR has a big lawn and a pond.
5. Our family likes to play on the SGS and slides in the park.
6. Please would you lay the table with knives and KS.
7. Last summer she was stung by a P in the garden.
8. Watch carefully and CH the ball when I throw it to you.
9. My father gave my mother a big bunch of FERS.
10. In spring, the field behind us is filled with EP and lambs.
11. My CIL is blunt and needs sharpening.
12. Don't FOR to bring your gym things tomorrow.
13. All the leaves are falling off the trees and HES.
14. Climbing steep HS can make you puff.
15. Dad is PAING the bathroom blue.

TEST 8: Coded Sequences and Logic 1

Fill in the missing letters and numbers. The alphabet has been written out to help you. A B C D E F G H I J K L M N O P Q R S T U V W X Y Z

Example: AB is to CD as PQ is to RS.

1 PN is to LJ as HF is to _____.
2 16a is to 14b as 12c is to _____.
3 ABD is to EFH as IJL is to _____.
4 K1L is to M2N as O3P is to _____.

If a = 8, b = 2, c = 9 and d = 3, find the value of:

5 a + c + d = _____
6 2b + 2d = _____
7 3c − a = _____
8 (c − a) + d = _____
9 a + b + c + d = _____

If e = 2, f = 3, g = 4, h = 6 and j = 10, find the value of the following calculations. Write the answer as a letter.

10 2f − e = _____
11 (h + j) − ef = _____
12 2j − 3h = _____
13 2e + 2f = _____
14 5g − (j + 3e) = _____
15 (4e + 3g) − (j + g) = _____

Total _____

TEST 9: Coded Sequences and Logic 2

If the code for BEWARE is ZKPMHK, code and decode these words.

1 BEAR _____
2 RAW _____
3 BREW _____
4 ZMHK _____
5 PKMH _____

Here are four number codes: 7619 4613 1993 9674
Match them to the words below and then work out the missing code.

6 HAND _____
7 EACH _____
8 CANE _____
9 ACHE _____
10 NEED _____

If the code for:

11 TREAD is 67912, what is the code for DATE? _____
12 BEAST is FJODV, what is the code for BATS? _____
13 SLIME is BRPYX, what is the code for MILE? _____
14 PAINT is 35968, what is 3968? _____
15 THEME is $ + = * =, what is * = = $? _____

Time for a break! Go to Puzzle Page 40

Total _____

TEST 10: **Coded Sequences and Logic 3**

Test time:

Anne and Tom are wearing jeans. Anne and Billie have pink tops.
Stan and Billie are wearing tracksuit bottoms. Stan and Tom have blue tops.

1 Who is wearing tracksuit bottoms and a pink top? _____
2 Is Stan wearing a blue top and jeans? _____
3 What is Anne wearing with her pink top? _____

My bus should have arrived at 10:10. It is 15 minutes late.

4 What time is it now? _____

The bus waited at the bus stop for 5 minutes before leaving, and the journey took 20 minutes.

5 What time did I arrive at my destination? _____

The houses on one side of a street are even numbers from 2 to 20. On the other side they are odd numbers from 1 to 19. 1 is opposite 2, 3 is opposite 4 and so on. What number house is:

6 opposite 5? ____   7 between 13 and 17? ____   8 opposite 11? ____

Jake and Lewis own football boots. Stuart and Lewis own rugby boots.
Jake and Pete have cricket boots. Pete and Stuart have tennis shoes.

9   Who has tennis shoes and cricket boots? _____
10 Who has rugby boots and football boots? _____

A roasting joint weights 2kg. It takes 45 minutes a kilogram to cook and must be done by 1pm. The potatoes will take 70 minutes and must be ready at the same time.

11–13 How long will the joint take to cook?   ____ hr ____ mins
       When should the food be put in the oven?   joint ____   potatoes ____

The day before yesterday was Wednesday. What is:

14 today? _____   15 the day after tomorrow? _____

9

Total

TEST 11: **Mixed**

Test time: 0 | 5 | 10 minutes

Rearrange the muddled letters in capitals to make a proper word. The answer will complete the sentence sensibly.

Example: A BEZAR is an animal with stripes.   ZEBRA

1 I have to go back to the STINTED for a filling.   _____
2 David skilfully kicked the LLOBFATO.   _____
3 In the MERUSM holidays we are going to France.   _____
4 I like to watch the lambs GINYALP in the fields.   _____
5 Let's cross the road on the NALIPEC crossing.   _____

Underline the pair of words most opposite in meaning.

Example: cup, mug   coffee, milk   <u>hot, cold</u>

6   frost, snow   fresh, ripe   salty, sweet
7   even, equal   flexible, rigid   dark, shade
8   ghost, train   fail, pass   speak, talk
9   sensible, foolish crack, burst   rapid, fast
10 by, with   to, from   because, also

Solve each question by working out the code.

11 If the code for HOUSE is DRFPL, what is the code for SHOE?   _____
12 If the code for SHAME is 70832, what is the code for MESH?   _____
13 If the code for GREAT is DFMCV, what is the code for TEAR?   _____
14 If the code for RIGHT is < ^ / # > , what is / < ^ > ?   _____
15 If the code for BLAST is & * $ ^ %, what is % $ ** ?   _____

10

Total

TEST 12: **Mixed**

Find the letter which will end the first word and start the second word.

Example: peac (h) ome

1 bro (___) and

2 mic (___) nds

3 pur (___) isk

4 kin (___) row

5 for (___) ish

Underline the number that completes each sequence.

6 40 is to 20 as 30 is to (20, 60, 15).

7 19 is to 17 as 35 is to (33, 37, 36).

8 5 is to 20 as 6 is to (10, 24, 18).

9 111 is to 222 as 333 is to (555, 444, 33).

10 11 is to 22 as 7 is to (14, 19, 77).

In each line, underline the word which has its letters in alphabetical order.

11 fever   doubt   most   roof

12 baby   pray   take   foot

13 bitten   know   farm   daisy

14 birth   whole   blast   adder

15 slab   raid   flop   dark

TEST 13: Mixed

Find and underline the two words which need to change places for each sentence to make sense.

Example: She went to <u>letter</u> the <u>write</u>.

1. The little waves bobbed on the boat.
2. I am so sleepy that I feel really tired.
3. That woman is wearing not a coat.
4. There was a rumble of storm as the thunder broke.
5. Please help your meal with the mother.

Change one word so that the sentence makes sense. Underline the word you are taking out and write your new word on the line.

Example: I waited in line to buy a <u>book</u> to see the film. __ticket__

6. Please close the window, as we need some fresh air in the room. _____
7. As the road was icy and dangerous, Dad drove fast. _____
8. The postman emptied the postbox and put the carrots in his sack. _____
9. Hurry up or we will be early for the bus. _____
10. In Spring, the days start to get shorter and warmer. _____

Underline one word in the brackets which is the most opposite in meaning to the word in capitals.

Example: WIDE (broad   vague   long   <u>narrow</u>   motorway)

11. COOL   (distant   frosty   icy   cold   warm)
12. DANGER   (safety   risk   peril   accident   road)
13. CLIMB   (ascend   mountain   descend   ladder   stairs)
14. EXTREME (slight   great   serious   sports   maximum)
15. DEPART   (appear   go   depend   arrive   exceed)

Test 14: Mixed

Remove one letter from the word in capitals to leave a new word. The meaning of the new word is given in the clue.

Example: AUNT   an insect   ___ant___

1 WITCH   accompanying   _____
2 STABLE   not fresh   _____
3 SOFTEN   many times   _____
4 HARMFUL   amount you can carry _____
5 MOTHER   alternative   _____

Find the four-letter word hidden at the end of one word and the beginning of the next word. The order of the letters may not be changed.

Example: The children had ba<u>ts and</u> balls.   ___sand___

6 Please close the middle window.   _____
7 The baby monkey scampered up the tree.   _____
8 Kittens can be quite playful.   _____
9 A little after four o'clock, he left.   _____
10 Wendy and Sarah are coming as well.   _____

If the code for TRACTOR is WPFZWBP, what are the codes for the following words?

11 CART   _____
12 ROAR   _____
13 TACT   _____

Using the same code, decode these:

14 ZBFW   _____
15 WPBW   _____

TEST 15: **Mixed**

Test time: 0 — 5 — 10 minutes

Rearrange the muddled words in capital letters so that each sentence makes sense.

Example: There are sixty SNODCES __seconds__ in a UTMINE __minute__.

1–3 I am GIVANS _____ my TCPOKE _____ money to buy a new CYLBCEI _____ .

4–5 Don't CHOUT _____ that dog; it may TIEB _____.

Read the school timetable, and then work out how many minutes each of the following activities takes.

Assembly   9:00
Maths   9:20
English   10:00
Reading   10:45
Break   11:00

6 Assembly _____ minutes   **8** English _____ minutes
7 Maths   _____ minutes   **9** Reading _____ minutes

I have 50p more than my sister, who has 80p less than my brother. My brother has £5.50.

10 How much does my sister have? _____

11 How much do I have? _____

Underline two words, one from each group, that go together to form a new word. The word in the first group always comes first.

Example: (hand, <u>green</u>, for)   (light, <u>house</u>, sure)

12 (inter, ball, post)   (erupt, track, net)

13 (rain, suit, put)   (able, box, thing)

14 (sail, wasp, climb)   (or, up, bee)

15 (hard, my, be)   (time, bed, hind)

Total

TEST 16: **Mixed**

Test time: 0 5 10 minutes

Underline the two words, one from each group, which are the most opposite in meaning.

Example: (dawn, <u>early</u>, wake) (<u>late</u>, stop, sunrise)

1 (still, cold, wet)   (chilly, quiet, dry)
2 (hard, cap, pillow)   (soft, hat, bed)
3 (change, shiny, coin)   (money, dull, safe)
4 (circle, add, multiply)   (line, number, divide)
5 (save, find, hide)   (conceal, place, protect)

Look at these groups of words.
Group A: MALE   Group B: FEMALE
Choose the correct group for each of the following words. Write in the letter.

6 girl   ____
7 bull   ____
8 uncle   ____
9 matron   ____
10 father   ____

Give the missing numbers and letters in the following sequences.
The alphabet has been written out to help you.

A B C D E F G H I J K L M N O P Q R S T U V W X Y Z

Example: CQ   DQ   EP   FP   <u>GO</u>

11 ZY   XW   VU   TS   ____   PO
12 ____ bN   cM   dL   eK   fJ
13 4H   7G   4F   7E   4D   ____
14 2X   4W   ____ 8U   10T   12S
15 QR   ____ QT   QU   QV   QW

15

Time for a break! Go to Puzzle Page 40

Total

TEST 17: **Mixed**

If a = 2, b = 5, c = 10, d = 4 and e = 3, find the value of the following calculations. Write the answer as a letter.

1   2a + 2e =   _____
2   de − c =   _____
3   bc − cd =   _____
4   5b − 2c =   _____
5   (b + d + e) − c =   _____

Fill in the crosswords so that all the given words are included.
You have been given one letter as a clue in each crossword.

6, 7, 8, 9

| PARK | KING | SMUG | ATOM | STEP | NICE | FISH | THAT |
| PEEL | LUNG | TART | TANG | PINK | PASS | WINE | NEXT |

Complete the following sentences by selecting the most sensible word from each group of words given in the brackets. Underline the words selected.

Example: The (<u>children</u>, books, foxes) carried the (houses, <u>books</u>, steps) home from the (greengrocer, <u>library</u>, factory).

10   The (green, tiny, clean) (mouse, house, stone) scampered through the (happy, tall, metal) grass.

11   Dragons are said to have (short, scaly, slow) skin, a long (list, tail, step) and to (breathe, eat, climb) fire.

12   Neeta put (in, away, up) her (elephants, books, rocks) and went (on, out, by) for break.

13   If we (eat, walk, beat) over the common, we will get to the (swings, pencil, picture) where we can (play, fight, snow).

14   For (lunch, bucket, lessons) we had (seaside, sausages, paper), chips and (traffic, salad, rulers).

15   The (imaginary, happy, tattered) (book, scarecrow, postcard) frightened the birds away from the (library, fridge, field).

16

Total

Test 18: Mixed

Fill in the missing numbers and letters in each sequence.

Example: 2   4   6   8   __10__

1	15	18	___	24	27	30
2	5	10	20	40	___	160
3	6.5	7.0	7.5	8.0	___	9.0
4	1J1	2K2	3L3	___	5N5	6O6
5	5	6	8	11	15	___

Add one letter to the word given in capital letters to make a new word. The meaning of the new word is given in the clue.

Example: PLAN   simple   __plain__

6	ALL	tumble	_____
7	PICK	stab with a pin	_____
8	OUR	tip out	_____
9	STEAM	a little river	_____
10	PAY	worship	_____

If these words were placed in alphabetical order, which word would come last? Underline the word.

11	planet	space	rocket	moon	world
12	rabbit	horse	cat	dog	gerbil
13	traffic	tunnels	timber	thunder	tonsils
14	Friday	France	French	Frank	Freida
15	classical	claret	clarity	clarify	clarinet

17

Test 19: Mixed

Rearrange the muddled words in capital letters so that each sentence makes sense.

Example: There are sixty SNODCES __seconds__ in a UTMINE __minute__.

1–2 It is time to put on your STOAC _____ and go DEOTUIS _____ to play.

3–5 To reach the shops, you must turn GITRH _____ and walk ASTIRTHG _____ down the ETREST _____ to the end.

Complete the following sentences in the best way by choosing one word from each set of brackets.

Example: Tall is to (tree, <u>short</u>, colour) as narrow is to (thin, white, <u>wide</u>).

6   Quick is to (slow, fast, yellow) as high is to (hill, low, green).

7   Pick is to (fruit, shovel, choose) as climb is to (descend, rise, steep).

8   Smooth is to (soft, skin, rough) as calm is to (boat, sunny, stormy).

9   Monday is to (yesterday, Tuesday, March) as Saturday is to (weekend, holiday, Sunday).

10 Paw is to (dog, toe, claw) as hoof is to (horse, shoe, kick).

These words have been written in code but the codes are not under the correct words. Find the correct code for each word.

STOP	POST	PORT	TRIP
7931	1657	5761	1697

11   STOP _____

12   POST _____

13   PORT _____

14   TRIP _____

Using the same code, decode:

15   51697 _____

TEST 20: **Mixed**

Test time: 0 — 5 — 10 minutes

Underline one word in the brackets which is the most opposite in meaning to the word in capitals.

Example: WIDE   (broad   vague   long   <u>narrow</u>   motorway)

1   DISPLAY   (hide   show   present   wall   picture)
2   MERRY   (joyful   Christmas   gloomy   jolly   full)
3   PRESENT   (gift   wrap   here   absent   leave)
4   SECURE   (sound   safe   locked   guard   unsafe)
5   STRIPED   (patterned   plain   marked   pyjamas   tie)

Find the three-letter word which can be added to the letters in capitals to make a new word. The new word will complete the sentence sensibly.

Example: The cat sprang onto the MO.   _____USE_____

6   The wind blew the SUNFLRS over in her garden.   _____
7   Take your muddy boots off before you tread on the CAR.   _____
8   After school, our CHER marks our books.   _____
9   The fairy godmother waved her magic W.   _____
10   His THBRUSH and toothpaste are on the shelf.   _____

Choose the word or phrase that makes each sentence true.

Example: A LIBRARY always has (posters, carpet, <u>books</u>, DVDs, stairs).

11   A DOG always has a (dinner, collar, nose, bone, lead).
12   A ROOM always has (a carpet, furniture, pictures, walls, a fire).
13   A WOOD always has (trees, leaves, squirrels, paths, grass).
14   A BOTTLE always has (glass, milk, wine, sides, a straw).
15   A SHOE always has (a sole, laces, polish, an owner, a sock).

19

Total

Test 21: Mixed

Change the first word of the third pair in the same way as the other pairs to give a new word.

Example: bind, hind   bare, hare   but, __hut__

1. time, tame   wish, wash   stiff, _____
2. flame, fame   crane, cane   plain, _____
3. plug, gulp   doom, mood   dial, _____
4. bite, white   binge, whinge   bat, _____
5. meal, male   veal, vale   steal, _____

Underline the two words which are the odd ones out in the following groups of words.

Example: black <u>king</u> purple green <u>house</u>

6. foal   calf   beetle   duckling   wasp
7. many   some   lots   numerous   few
8. sum   add   metre   subtract   divide
9. line   talk   chat   row   discuss
10. anger   happy   rage   fury   laugh

Give the missing numbers and letters in the following sequences. The alphabet has been written out to help you.

A B C D E F G H I J K L M N O P Q R S T U V W X Y Z

Example: CQ   DQ   EP   FP   <u>GO</u>

11. NM   LK   JI   ____   FE   DC
12. OPA   QRA   STA   UVA   WXA   ____
13. ab12   cd23   ____   gh45   ij56   kl67
14. 9OP   8QR   9ST   8UV   ____   8YZ
15. ABB   ____   ADD   AEE   AFF   AGG

Test 22: **Mixed**

Test time: 0 — 5 — 10 minutes

Find a word that can be put in front of each of the following words to make new, compound words.

Example: CAST   FALL   WARD   POUR   __DOWN__

1	WRITING	CUFF	SOME	SHAKE	_____
2	SURFING	SWEPT	MILL	SCREEN	_____
3	SHEET	SHOP	MAN	OUT	_____
4	SCOTCH	FLY	FINGERS	CUP	_____
5	LAND	LIGHT	WAY	BROW	_____

From the information below, work out which flavours of chocolates are in each of the spaces in the chocolate box.

TOP

NOUGAT	A	B
C	TOFFEE	D
E	F	COFFEE CUP

BOTTOM

The Nut Cluster is next to the Strawberry Delight but directly below the Chocolate Almond.

The Chocolate Log is closer to the top than the Nut Cluster but directly below the Tangerine Surprise, which is next to the Caramel Melt.

6	Nut Cluster	_____	9	Chocolate Log	_____
7	Strawberry Delight	_____	10	Tangerine Surprise	_____
8	Chocolate Almond	_____	11	Caramel Melt	_____

Fill in the crosswords so that all the given words are included. You have been given one letter as a clue in each crossword.

12
ONLY   GOOD
GAME   MALE

13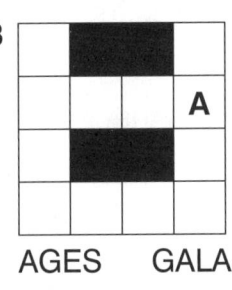
AGES   GALA
SAFE   HAZE

14
HUSH   BATH
OWLS   BOOK

15
JUMP   TURN
ZULU   SNIP

21

Total

Test 23: Mixed

Find and underline the two words which need to change places for each sentence to make sense.

Example: She went to <u>letter</u> the <u>write</u>.

1. Come in quietly as the baby is asleep fast.
2. The pub sign swung as it creaked in the wind.
3. I have right my books in the room on the left.
4. We are buying our car and selling a new one.
5. Please put the rail back on the towel.

Change one word so that the sentence makes sense. Underline the word you are taking out and write your new word on the line.

Example: I waited in line to buy a <u>book</u> to see the film.   ___ticket___

6. As it is raining, we will stay outside and keep dry. _____
7. Fish are able to breathe out of water. _____
8. Tears poured down her face as she was so happy. _____
9. The dog mooed happily when she saw her calf. _____
10. Lara fell up and cut her knee. _____

Solve each question by working out the code.

11. If the code for CHOIR is ~ # £ @ *, what is the code for RICH? _____
12. If the code for BASIN is GHYWC, what is the code for BINS? _____
13. If the code for TIGHT is 57935, what is the code for HIGH? _____
14. If the code for TRAIN is c b s l d, what is b s d c? _____
15. If the code for FLOWN is − = + × > what is × + + = ? _____

22

Total

Bond 10 Minute Tests 8–9 years: Verbal Reasoning

Answers

Test 1: Sorting Words 1

1. story, tale
2. sight, vision
3. free, release
4. dish, bowl
5. finish, halt
6. nervous
7. chief
8. beneath
9. changeable
10. burn
11. fib
12. capture
13. lady
14. blend
15. attack

Test 2: Selecting Words 1

1. h
2. y
3. b
4. m
5. a
6. o
7. k
8. s
9. p
10. r
11. e
12. b
13. f
14. z
15. e

Test 3: Sorting and Selecting Words

1. late, early
2. little, large
3. break, mend
4. below, above
5. calm, rough
6. improve, better
7. attempt, try
8. stay, remain
9. hard, difficult
10. hurl, fling
11. win
12. heat
13. cane
14. beach
15. light

Test 4: Selecting Words 2

1. forehead
2. chatterbox
3. highlight
4. mushroom
5. upset
6. carpet
7. clapping
8. night, bed, teeth
9. coat, blue, red
10. hungry, dog, bone
11. rusty, gate, squeaked
12. rained, deep, playground
13. rocket, sky, station
14. uncle, mother's, brother
15. down, fragrant, garden

Test 5: Anagrams 1

1. FIREWORK
2. SUNDAY
3. MOWING
4. QUIET
5. PICTURE
6. STIR
7. PASS
8. MORE
9. FIRE
10. ITEM
11. REST
12. FOAL
13. VEST
14. PLAN
15. KISS

Test 6: Anagrams 2

1. brown
2. chest
3. August
4. trample
5. produce
6. abbot
7. bossy
8. ghost
9. glory
10. lost
11. added
12. faced
13. bead
14. cafe
15. deaf

Test 7: Anagrams 3

1. ALL
2. RAN
3. TEA
4. DEN
5. WIN
6. FOR
7. WAS
8. CAT
9. LOW
10. SHE
11. PEN
12. GET
13. BUS
14. ILL
15. TIN

Test 8: Coded Sequences and Logic 1

1. DB
2. 10d
3. MNP
4. Q4R
5. 20
6. 10
7. 19
8. 4
9. 22
10. g
11. j
12. e
13. j
14. g
15. h

Test 9: Coded Sequences and Logic 2

1. ZKMH
2. HMP
3. ZHKP
4. BARE
5. WEAR
6. 4613
7. 9674
8. 7619
9. 6749
10. 1993
11. 2169
12. FOVD
13. YPRX
14. PINT
15. MEET

Test 10: Coded Sequences and Logic 3

1. Billie
2. no
3. jeans
4. 10:25
5. 10:50
6. 6
7. 15
8. 12
9. Pete
10. Lewis
11. 1 hr 30 mins
12. 11:30
13. 11:50
14. Friday
15. Sunday

Test 11: Mixed

1. DENTIST
2. FOOTBALL
3. SUMMER
4. PLAYING
5. PELICAN
6. salty, sweet
7. flexible, rigid
8. fail, pass
9. sensible, foolish
10. to, from
11. PDRL
12. 3270
13. VMCF
14. GRIT
15. TALL

Test 12: Mixed

1. w
2. e
3. r
4. g
5. d
6. 15
7. 33
8. 24
9. 444
10. 14
11. most
12. foot
13. know
14. adder
15. flop

Test 13: Mixed

1. waves, boat
2. sleepy, tired
3. wearing, not
4. storm, thunder
5. meal, mother
6. close, open
7. fast, slowly
8. carrots, letters
9. early, late
10. shorter, longer
11. warm
12. safety
13. descend
14. slight
15. arrive

Test 14: Mixed

1. with
2. stale
3. often
4. armful
5. other
6. them
7. keys
8. scan
9. leaf
10. hare
11. ZFPW
12. PBFP
13. WFZW
14. COAT
15. TROT

Bond 10 Minute Tests 8–9 years: Verbal Reasoning

Test 15: Mixed
1 saving
2 pocket
3 bicycle
4 touch
5 bite
6 20
7 40
8 45
9 15
10 £4.70
11 £5.20
12 internet
13 suitable
14 sailor
15 behind

Test 16: Mixed
1 wet, dry
2 hard, soft
3 shiny, dull
4 multiply, divide
5 find, conceal
6 B
7 A
8 A
9 B
10 A
11 RQ
12 aO
13 7C
14 6V
15 QS

Test 17: Mixed
1 c
2 a
3 c
4 b
5 a

10 tiny, mouse, tall
11 scaly, tail, breathe
12 away, books, out
13 walk, swings, play
14 lunch, sausages, salad
15 tattered, scarecrow, field

Test 18: Mixed
1 21
2 80
3 8.5
4 4M4
5 20
6 fall
7 prick
8 pour
9 stream
10 pray
11 world
12 rabbit
13 tunnels
14 Friday
15 classical

Test 19: Mixed
1 coats
2 outside
3 right
4 straight
5 street
6 slow, low
7 choose, rise
8 rough, stormy
9 Tuesday, Sunday
10 dog, horse
11 5761
12 1657
13 1697
14 7931
15 SPORT

Test 20: Mixed
1 hide
2 gloomy
3 absent
4 unsafe
5 plain
6 OWE
7 PET
8 TEA
9 AND
10 TOO
11 nose
12 walls
13 trees
14 sides
15 a sole

Test 21: Mixed
1 staff
2 pain
3 laid
4 what
5 stale
6 beetle, wasp
7 some, few
8 sum, metre
9 line, row
10 happy, laugh
11 HG
12 YZA
13 ef34
14 9WX
15 ACC

Test 22: Mixed
1 HAND
2 WIND
3 WORK
4 BUTTER
5 HIGH
6 E
7 F
8 C
9 D
10 B
11 A

12
G	O	O	D
A		N	
M	A	L	E
E		Y	

14
B	A	T	H
O		U	
O	W	L	S
K		H	

13
A		H	
G	A	L	A
E		Z	
S	A	F	E

15
T		J	
Z	U	L	U
R		M	
S	N	I	P

Test 23: Mixed
1 asleep, fast
2 swung, creaked
3 right, left
4 buying, selling
5 rail, towel
6 outside, inside
7 able, unable
8 happy, sad
9 dog, cow
10 up, down
11 * @ ~ #
12 GWCY
13 3793
14 RANT
15 WOOL

Test 24: Mixed
1 lie, truth
2 backwards, forwards
3 dawn, dusk
4 broad, narrow
5 far, near
6 8
7 12
8 20
9 t
10 t
11 chief
12 labelled
13 decide
14 dabble
15 jackal

Test 25: Mixed
1 LAP, PAL
2 DRAW, WARD
3 APT, TAP
4 LEFT, FELT
5 BEARD, BREAD
6 BEAR
7 POOR
8 PIES
9 WIDE
10 HAZY
11 outside, under
12 large, little
13 head, finger
14 pen, brush
15 firm, smooth

A2

Bond 10 Minute Tests 8–9 years: Verbal Reasoning

Test 26: Mixed

1 peculiar
2 annoy
3 direct
4 glance
5 pour
6 four
7 wine
8 hate
9 nest
10 they
11 tank
12 angle
13 swam
14 sight
15 step

Test 27: Mixed

1 MINE
2 SLOT
3 BASH
4 LUNG
5 BEAR
6 garden, letter
7 oval, circle
8 one, two
9 money, shop
10 dark, tough
11 door, toilet
12 time, just
13 feet, shoes
14 park, storm
15 Autumn, leaves

Test 28: Mixed

1 VX
2 13G
3 CB
4 G4H
5 wxy
6 f
7 b
8 n
9 e
10 c
11 lane
12 trainer
13 orange
14 pen
15 foot

Test 29: Mixed

1 HPQJ
2 CPQH
3 QXHR
4 QPHZ
5 BALL
6 peel, skin
7 reply, respond
8 giggle, chuckle
9 gather, assemble
10 entire, complete
11 boring
12 bush
13 wolf
14 from
15 star

Test 30: Mixed

1 19
2 17
3 12
4 20
5 3
6 THE
7 ARC
8 HUT
9 ASH
10 AIR
11 tent
12 wasp
13 first
14 plain
15 steep

Test 31: Mixed

1 5493
2 2745
3 2453
4 TEAM
5 MATE
6 legs
7 a mattress
8 pages
9 wheels
10 food
11 PILE
12 FLAP
13 WADE
14 FOOL
15 MICE

Test 32: Mixed

1 h
2 t
3 o
4 w
5 k
6 tour
7 vest
8 card
9 dove
10 than
11 grin
12 blade
13 nose
14 drain
15 roast

Test 33: Mixed

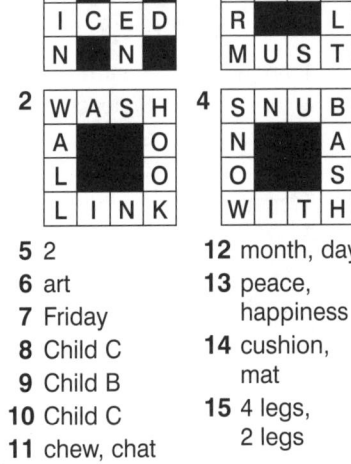

5 2
6 art
7 Friday
8 Child C
9 Child B
10 Child C
11 chew, chat
12 month, day
13 peace, happiness
14 cushion, mat
15 4 legs, 2 legs

Test 34: Mixed

1 11
2 75
3 8
4 9
5 10y
6 Leeds, London
7 left, dark
8 cloud, basin
9 mirror, picture
10 daughter, mother
11 LIFE
12 EYE
13 SOME
14 RAIN
15 FINGER

Test 35: Mixed

1 APE, PEA
2 LAIR, RAIL
3 TASTE, STATE
4 REAR, RARE
5 ITS, SIT

6

D		S	
E	D	I	T
S		E	
K	N	O	W

8

	W		S
B	E	L	T
	L		U
P	L	A	N

7

J	A	M	S
A		O	
Z	O	O	M
Z		E	

9

R	A	C	K
A		I	
N	O	T	E
G		Y	

10 controlled, passed, goal
11 listen, instructions, shouted
12 that, iceberg, water
13 sheep, horns, not
14 finished, writing, play
15 school, learning, life

Test 36: Mixed

1 OWN
2 YES
3 RAN
4 OUR
5 TEN
6 cats
7 dogs
8 5
9 others
10 fish
11 20
12 bathroom
13 bitten
14 knowledge
15 quicksand

Test 37: Mixed

5 8
6 13
7 19
8 9
9 6
10 4
11 B
12 A
13 B
14 A
15 C

A3

Bond 10 Minute Tests 8–9 years: Verbal Reasoning

Test 38: Mixed

1 h
2 p
3 d
4 s
5 k
6 breadth, width
7 save, conserve
8 tint, hue
9 knot, fasten
10 smooth, silky
11 talk
12 low
13 sandwich
14 screw
15 night

Test 39: Mixed

1 13
2 3
3 28
4 44
5 20
6 hour
7 stop
8 land
9 seal
10 fern
11 sneer
12 treat
13 stand
14 slide
15 swoon

Test 40: Mixed

1 LAKE
2 FURL
3 PACK
4 BEAT
5 FOOL
6 SON
7 BOW
8 OUT
9 ATE
10 CAR
11 VX
12 2DX
13 JIL
14 ghi
15 9AC

Puzzle ❶

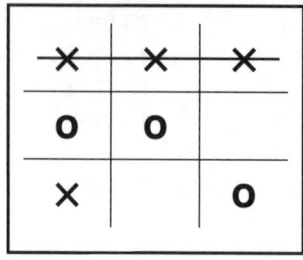

Puzzle ❷

wand	kill	reel
dart	laid	loaf
trip	down	flip
park	near	prow

Puzzle ❸

1 angle
2 ropes
3 broad
4 cheat
5 spear
6 gable
7 straw
8 peach
9 state
10 table
11 worth
12 stale

Puzzle ❹

W	EAR	AIL	TOP	HIP	ASH
	BID	HEN	ALL	ARM	KIT
S	OAK	JAR	CAN	TAR	CAR
	WAN	TOW	PIT	ALL	OWL
F	ATE	ILL	AIR	ITS	OUR
	OAR	ICE	ASH	FOX	MOW
R	EEL	HOP	AIL	ATE	EAR
	OAR	ICE	ASH	SEA	MOW

Puzzle ❺

1 February
2 December

A4

TEST 24: Mixed

Underline the two words, one from each group, which are the most opposite in meaning.

Example: (dawn, <u>early</u>, wake) (<u>late</u>, stop, sunrise)

1 (sleep, lie, work)   (night, snore, truth)
2 (backwards, down, beside)   (forwards, inside, across)
3 (moon, light, dawn)   (day, dusk, night)
4 (talk, broad, tall)   (chatter, wide, narrow)
5 (far, steady, closed)   (distant, near, firm)

If q = 2, r = 3, s = 5 and t = 10, find the value of:

6 (r + t) − s = _____
7 6q = _____
8 q + r + s + t = _____

Now give the answers of these calculations as letters:

9   sq = _____
10 q + r + s = _____

Underline the word in each line which uses only letters from the first 12 letters of the alphabet. The alphabet has been written out to help you.

A B C D E F G H I J K L M N O P Q R S T U V W X Y Z

11 basket   lettuce   flannel   chief
12 labelled   bridge   chimney   fussy
13 dragon   decide   flavour   current
14 bitten   joker   dabble   laugh
15 lantern   casket   jackal   height

Time for a break! Go to Puzzle Page 41

Total

Test 25: **Mixed**

Test time: 0 — 5 — 10 minutes

Underline the two words which are made from the same letters.

Example: TAP PET <u>TEA</u> POT <u>EAT</u>

1 LAP PAW PAL SAP SAW
2 CARD DRAW CROW WARD WORD
3 FAT TAR FAR APT TAP
4 LEFT FLED FELT FEED DEFT
5 DREAD BEARD TREAT TRADE BREAD

Look at the first group of three words. The word in the middle has been made from the other two words. Complete the second group of three words in the same way, making a new word in the middle.

Example: PAIN INTO TOOK   ALSO SOON ONLY

6 DENT DESK SKIP   BEAN beach ARCH
7 FELT FOOT BOOK   PEAR ____ SOOT
8 LIFE LIPS TAPS   PILE Pile EYES
9 GIFT GIVE VEST   WISH ____ DEFY
10 MILK MOON SOON   HIGH ____ LAZY

Complete the following sentences in the best way by choosing one word from each set of brackets.

Example: Tall is to (tree, <u>short</u>, colour) as narrow is to (thin, white, <u>wide</u>).

11 Inside is to (house, garden, outside) as over is to (above, under, near).

12 Big is to (elephant, large, tiny) as small is to (little, pain, quick).

13 Hair is to (head, ribbon, long) as nail is to (wood, hammer, finger).

14 Ink is to (pencil, word, pen) as paint is to (brush, colour, red).

15 Slippery is to (eel, firm, mud) as bumpy is to (smooth, road, track).

24

Total

Test 26: Mixed

Underline the word in the brackets closest in meaning to the word in capitals.

Example: UNHAPPY (unkind   death   laughter   <u>sad</u>   friendly)

1. STRANGE   (ordinary   usual   extra   visitor   peculiar)
2. VEX   (tired   annoy   please   wonder   chew)
3. STRAIGHT   (curved   narrow   direct   lined   crooked)
4. PEEP   (peck   glide   stare   horn   glance)
5. TIP   (pour   catch   money   bottom   bin)

Find the four-letter word hidden at the end of one word and the beginning of the next word. The order of the letters may not be changed.

Example: The children had ba<u>ts and</u> balls. ___sand___

6. Please take those coats off our chairs. _____
7. Ravi is so quick, he will win every race. _____
8. Sarah ate a whole tin of toffees. _____
9. One star is shining particularly brightly. _____
10. Leaves are blowing in the air in the yard. _____

Remove one letter from the word in capitals to leave a new word. The meaning of the new word is given in the clue.

Example: AUNT   an insect   ___ant___

11. THANK   container   _____
12. TANGLE   corner   _____
13. SWARM   bathed   _____
14. SLIGHT   vision   _____
15. STEEP   tread   _____

TEST 27: **Mixed**

Test time: 0 — 5 — 10 minutes

Change the first word into the last word, by changing one letter at a time and making a new, different word in the middle.

Example: CASE   __CASH__   LASH

1   WINE   _____   MINT
2   SLIT   _____   SLOW
3   WASH   _____   BATH
4   RUNG   _____   LONG
5   BOAR   _____   BEER

Underline the two words which are the odd ones out in the following groups of words.

Example: black   <u>king</u>   purple   green   <u>house</u>

6   respect   garden   value   prize   letter
7   square   rectangle hexagon   oval   circle
8   one   two   third   fourth   fifth
9   cost   expense   money   shop   price
10   dark   light   flimsy   delicate   tough

Find and underline the two words which need to change places for each sentence to make sense.

Example: She went to <u>letter</u> the <u>write</u>.

11   The door sign has fallen off the toilet.

12   You have arrived time in just for tea.

13   Why have you put your feet on the wrong shoes?

14   In a park, the storm bench was blown over.

15   The Autumn fall during the leaves.

26

Total

TEST 28: Mixed

Fill in the missing letters and numbers. The alphabet has been written out to help you.

A B C D E F G H I J K L M N O P Q R S T U V W X Y Z

Example: AB is to CD as PQ is to _RS_.

1 MO is to PR as SU is to _____.

2 19D is to 17E as 15F is to _____.

3 ML is to KJ as ED is to _____.

4 A1B is to C2D as E3F is to _____.

5 nop is to qrs as tuv is to _____.

Which one letter can be added to the front of all these words to make new words?

Example: _c_ are   _c_ at   _c_ rate   _c_ all

6   ___ arm   ___ attest   ___ ox   ___ ling
7   ___ rain   ___ right   ___ last   ___ lank
8   ___ ape   ___ ought   ___ ail   ___ ice
9   ___ ager   ___ mpty   ___ at   ___ yes
10 ___ limb   ___ rust   ___ rash   ___ lock

Underline the word in the brackets which goes best with the words given outside the brackets.

Example: word, paragraph, sentence   (pen, cap, <u>letter</u>, top, stop)

11 road, street, avenue   (town, lane, footpath, car, walk)

12 sandal, slipper, boot   (socks, close, person, hat, trainer)

13 melon, apple, strawberry   (orange, vegetables, meat, farm, garden)

14 ruler, rubber, pencil   (lesson, case, pen, book, school)

15 toes, ankle, heel   (son, hand, stocking, foot, glove)

TEST 29: **Mixed**   Test time: 0 — 5 — 10 minutes

These words have been written in code but the codes are not under the correct words. Match each word to the correct code.

   MILK   FILM   LAMB   LIMP
   QXHR   QPHZ   CPQH   HPQJ

1 MILK _____
2 FILM _____
3 LAMB _____
4 LIMP _____

Using the same code, decode:

5 RXQQ _____

Underline the pair of words most similar in meaning.

Example: come, go   <u>roam, wander</u>   fear, fare

6   pick, mix   forgive, forget   peel, skin
7   reply, respond   question, answer   ask, shout
8   laugh, cry   weeping, smiling   giggle, chuckle
9   collect, deliver take, away   gather, assemble
10 entrance, exit   entire, complete   play, ground

Change the first word of the third pair in the same way as the other pairs to give a new word.

Example: bind, hind   bare, hare   but, __hut__

11 comb, coming   town, towing   bore, _____
12 rust, rush   crust, crush   bust, _____
13 nuts, stun   drab, bard   flow, _____
14 loin, lion   silt, slit   form, _____
15 pillow, pill   milked, milk   starts, _____

Test 30: Mixed

If v = 3, w = 8, y = 5 and z = 7, find the value of:

1. vw − y = _____
2. 2y + z = _____
3. 3z − 3v = _____
4. w + y + z = _____
5. w − y = _____

Find the three-letter word which can be added to the letters in capitals to make a new word. The new word will complete the sentence sensibly.

Example: The cat sprang onto the MO. ___USE___

6. Put them on the table over RE please. _____
7. Simon is the postman who delivers letters and PELS in our street. _____
8. Our teacher likes us to S the door quietly, not slam it. _____
9. The children SPLED merrily in the puddles. _____
10. The old man sits in his favourite ARMCH by the fire. _____

Add one letter to the word given in capital letters to make a new word. The meaning of the new word is given in the clue.

Example: PLAN   simple   ___plain___

11. TEN   a cloth shelter   _____
12. WAS   an insect   _____
13. FIST   before second   _____
14. PLAN   not patterned   _____
15. STEP   high and sloping   _____

Test 31: Mixed

If the code for MARKET is 547932, what are the codes for the following words?

1. MAKE _____
2. TRAM _____
3. TAME _____

Using the same code, decode these:

4. 2345 _____
5. 5423 _____

Choose the word or phrase that makes each sentence true.

Example: A LIBRARY always has (posters, carpet, <u>books</u>, DVDs, stairs).

6. A BEETLE always has (legs, stripes, food, shelter, spots).
7. A BED always has (a duvet, pillows, pyjamas, a mattress, sheets).
8. A BOOK always has (a story, pictures, a bookshelf, a library, pages).
9. A CAR always has (a driver, passengers, a boot, wheels, four doors).
10. A GROCERY SHOP always has (a restaurant, clothes, food, flowers, a bakery).

Look at the first group of three words. The word in the middle has been made from the other two words. Complete the second group of three words in the same way, making a new word in the middle.

Example: PA<u>IN</u> <u>IN</u>TO <u>T</u>OOK ALSO <u>SOON</u> ONLY

11. BELT BEAN ANTS PICK _____ LEAN
12. QUIP QUAY BRAY FLEW _____ SWAP
13. JAMS JOIN COIN WEST _____ FADE
14. SPUN SOON WOOL FAIL _____ TOOK
15. KING KILT SALT MILK _____ FACE

Test 32: Mixed

Find the letter which will end the first word and start the second word.

Example: peac (h) ome

1. pat (___) ope
2. bel (___) han
3. her (___) nce
4. cla (___) ise
5. bac (___) ite

Find the four-letter word hidden at the end of one word and the beginning of the next word. The order of the letters may not be changed.

Example: The children had bat<u>s and</u> balls. ___sand___

6. All of us caught our balls. _____
7. The waves tossed the boat. _____
8. The old car door was very rusty. _____
9. The horse jumped over the fence. _____
10. Both animals were extremely fierce. _____

Underline the one word which **cannot be made** from the letters of the word in capital letters.

Example: STATIONERY   stones   tyres   ration   <u>nation</u>   noisy

11	THINKING	grin	king	thin	ink	hint
12	BATTLES	slate	bats	steal	blade	bleat
13	CUSHION	such	nose	coin	shun	chin
14	BIRTHDAY	dirt	yard	drab	bath	drain
15	HISTORY	story	shirt	roast	hoist	rosy

TEST 33: **Mixed**

Test time: 0　5　10 minutes

Fill in the crosswords so that all the given words are included.
You have been given one letter as a clue in each crossword.

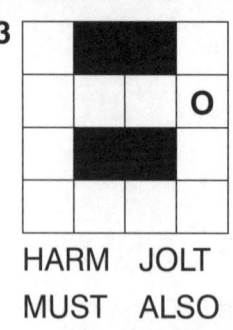
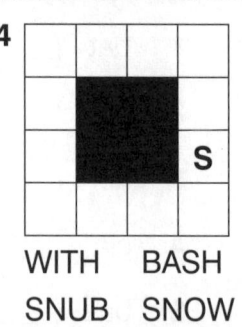

1 VEST SEEN
   VAIN ICED

2 WASH LINK
   HOOK WALL

3 HARM JOLT
   MUST ALSO

4 WITH BASH
   SNUB SNOW

Some children have after school activities.

Child A has ballet on Monday, dancing on Thursday and tennis on Saturday. Child B has scouts on Wednesday and football on Sunday. Child C has ballet on Monday, art on Tuesday, music on Thursday and athletics on Saturday. Child D has swimming on Monday, scouts on Wednesday and football on Sunday. Child E has swimming on Monday, dancing on Thursday and tennis on Saturday.

5 How many children play football? _____
6 Which activity takes place on Tuesday? _____
7 On which day is there no activity? _____
8 Which child has the most activities? _____
9 Which child has Mondays free but is busy on Sundays? _____
10 Which child does activities that none of the others do? _____

Complete the following sentences in the best way by choosing one word from each set of brackets.

Example: Tall is to (tree, <u>short</u>, colour) as narrow is to (thin, white, <u>wide</u>).

11 Bite is to (food, swallow, chew) as talk is to (phone, eat, chat).
12 February is to (winter, month, year) as Sunday is to (weekend, day, holiday).
13 War is to (peace, battle, fight) as sadness is to (happiness, rain, darkness).
14 Pillow is to (cushion, bed, feather) as rug is to (room, picture, mat).
15 Cat is to (whiskers, tail, 4 legs) as man is to (woman, 2 legs, arms).

32

TEST 34: **Mixed**

Test time: 0 — 5 — 10 minutes

Fill in the missing numbers and letters in each sequence.

Example: 2   4   6   8   __10__

1   7   ____   15   19   23   27
2   31   42   53   64   ____   86
3   2   4   ____   16   32   64
4   21   16   12   ____   7   6
5   ____   13x   16w   19v   22u   25t

Underline the two words which are the odd ones out in the following groups of words.

Example: black   <u>king</u>   purple   green   <u>house</u>

6   Wales   Leeds   London   Scotland   Ireland
7   right   left   fair   honest   dark
8   candle   lamp   torch   cloud   basin
9   mirror   newspaper   book   picture   magazine
10   son   daughter   grandfather   nephew   mother

Find a word that can be put in front of each of the following words to make new, compound words.

Example: CAST   FALL   WARD   POUR   __DOWN__

11   GUARD   BOAT   STYLE   TIME   _____
12   WITNESS   SHADOW   BROW   BALL   _____
13   THING   HOW   WHAT   BODY   _____
14   DROP   COAT   FOREST   BOW   _____
15   NAIL   PRINT   TIP   BOARD   _____

33

Total

TEST 35: **Mixed**

Test time: 0 — 5 — 10 minutes

Underline the two words which are made from the same letters.

Example: TAP   PET   <u>TEA</u>   POT   <u>EAT</u>

1 RAP   APE   PAT   PEA   TAR
2 NAIL   RAIN   LAIR   HAIR   RAIL
3 TASTE   TREAT   STATE   TOAST   TEASE
4 REAR   RAIN   NEAR   REAL   RARE
5 NET   ITS   TIN   SIT   SET

Fill in the crosswords so that all the given words are included.
You have been given one letter as a clue in each crossword.

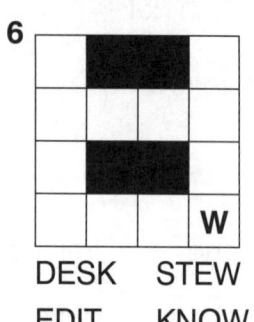

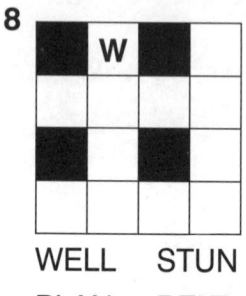

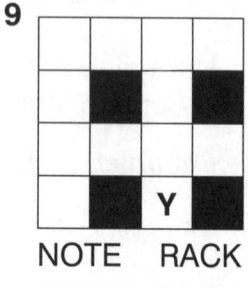

6 DESK   STEW
   EDIT   KNOW

7 SOME   JAMS
   JAZZ   ZOOM

8 WELL   STUN
   PLAN   BELT

9 NOTE   RACK
   CITY   RANG

Complete the following sentences by selecting the most sensible word from each group of words given in the brackets. Underline the words selected.

Example: The (<u>children</u>, books, foxes) carried the (houses, <u>books</u>, steps) home from the (greengrocer, <u>library</u>, factory).

10 Kieran skilfully (called, controlled, kissed) the ball and (passed, flew, pierced) it to Darren who scored a (look, goal, pigeon).

11 'Why can't you (listen, eat, climb) carefully to (table, instructions, pebbles)?' (shouted, dug, swam) Dad.

12 It is said (than, think, that) only one tenth of an (ice cream, icicle, iceberg) is visible above the (fire, earth, water) surface level.

13 Some (classrooms, sheep, jackets) have (horns, waterfalls, fences) but many do (knot, no, not).

14 When I had (started, wished, finished) (writing, eating, playing) my story, I went out to (cry, play, work).

15 At (school, hospital, pavement) we are (learning, eating, shouting) about the Romans and their way of (school, life, help) in Britain.

34

Total

TEST 36: Mixed

Find the three-letter word which can be added to the letters in capitals to make a new word. The new word will complete the sentence sensibly.

Example: The cat sprang onto the MO.   __USE__

1 Please sit D on that chair.
2 He has a kind face with big brown E.
3 Your GDMOTHER is taller than mine.
4 Driving on the motorway to London takes about half an H.
5 Gina's cat has just had KITS.

The chart below shows how many pets two classes have.

	DOGS	CATS	FISH	GERBILS	OTHERS	NONE
CLASS X	3	12	3	2	7	2
CLASS Y	7	9	6	0	11	3

6 Which pet is most popular of all?
7 Which pet is more popular in Class Y, dogs or fish?
8 How many children altogether have no pets?
9 Which column has the greatest number in Class Y?
10 Which pet is twice as popular in Class Y than Class X?
11 How many children altogether have gerbils and 'other' pets?

Underline two words, one from each group, that go together to form a new word. The word in the first group always comes first.

Example: (hand, <u>green</u>, for)   (light, <u>house</u>, sure)

12 (orange, bath, bubble)   (soap, sky, room)
13 (off, soft, bit)   (ten, win, bed)
14 (know, term, win)   (rim, ledge, side)
15 (slippery, quick, stony)   (rock, change, sand)

Test 37: Mixed

Test time: 0 – 5 – 10 minutes

Fill in the crosswords so that all the given words are included.
You have been given one letter as a clue in each crossword.

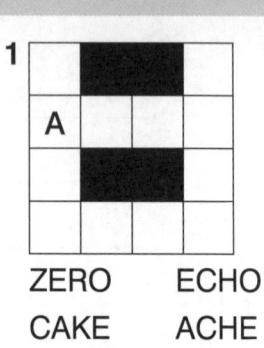

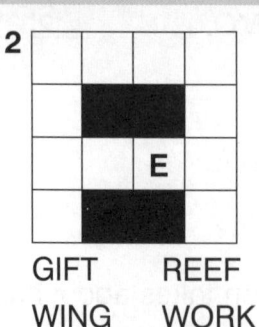

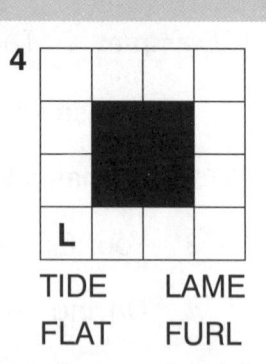

1 ZERO ECHO
    CAKE ACHE

2 GIFT REEF
    WING WORK

3 PLAY COSY
    BELL VETO

4 TIDE LAME
    FLAT FURL

The houses on one side of a street are even numbers from 2 to 20.
On the other side they are odd numbers from 1 to 19.
1 is opposite 2, 3 is opposite 4 and so on.

5   What number house is opposite 7?   _____
6   What number house is opposite 14?   _____
7   What number house is a higher number and next to 17?   _____
8   Which house is a lower number and opposite to 10?   _____

House number 3 and House number 4 have blue doors.
House number 4 and House number 5 have window boxes.
House number 3 and House number 6 have large door knockers.
Houses 5 and 6 have green doors.
Which house has:

9   a green door and a large door knocker?   _____
10 a blue door and a window box?   _____

Look at these groups of words.
Group A: ON LAND   Group B: ON WATER   Group C: IN THE AIR
Choose the correct group for each of the types of transport below.
Write in the letter.

11 boat   _____   14 van   _____
12 train   _____   15 helicopter   _____
13 ship   _____

TEST 38: Mixed

Which one letter can be added to the front of all these words to make new words?

Example: _c_ are   _c_ at   _c_ rate   _c_ all

1   ___ eel   ___ earth   ___ eat   ___ and
2   ___ ram   ___ lease   ___ ink   ___ itch
3   ___ evil   ___ ear   ___ ark   ___ rink
4   ___ port   ___ weep   ___ team   ___ tray
5   ___ nit   ___ ill   ___ not   ___ night

Underline the pair of words most similar in meaning.

Example: come, go   <u>roam, wander</u>   fear, fare

6   tall, thin   high, low   breadth, width
7   look, listen   save, conserve   rash, sensible
8   tint, hue   blue, colour   sky, sea
9   tie, laces   bind, weed   knot, fasten
10 soft, touch   smooth, silky   delicate, harsh

If these words were placed in alphabetical order, which would come second to last? Underline the word.

11 talk   converse   shout   yell   call
12 high   low   below   above   up
13 biscuit   cake   sandwich   cookie   tart
14 screw   nail   tack   pin   hammer
15 light   dark   night   day   sunshine

Test 39: Mixed

Underline the number that completes each sequence.

1. 21 is to 19 as 15 is to (13, 17, 11).
2. 8 is to 4 as 6 is to (12, 3, 18).
3. 13 is to 26 as 14 is to (27, 28, 18).
4. 77 is to 66 as 55 is to (44, 555, 11).
5. 1 is to 10 as 11 is to (16, 20, 2).

Find the four-letter word hidden at the end of one word and the beginning of the next word. The order of the letters may not be changed.

Example: The children had bat<u>s and</u> balls.   <u> sand </u>

6. Let's run and catch our bus.   _____
7. You must open all the windows.   _____
8. Paul and Adam liked the film too.   _____
9. Please allow enough time to get there.   _____
10. I definitely prefer nuts to raisins.   _____

Underline the one word which cannot be made from the letters of the word in capital letters.

Example: STATIONERY   stones   tyres   ration   <u>nation</u>   noisy

11	CORNERS	crone	rose	snore	sneer	corn
12	FEATHER	there	reef	treat	fear	heart
13	DUSTING	stand	gust	stud	sting	sung
14	SEASIDE	seed	slide	aside	dies	ease
15	WOODLAND	wool	load	wand	lawn	swoon

Test 40: Mixed

Change the first word into the last word, by changing one letter at a time and making a new, different word in the middle.

Example: CASE   CASH   LASH

1 WAKE   _____   LAME
2 HURL   _____   FURY
3 PICK   _____   BACK
4 FEAT   _____   BOAT
5 TOOL   _____   FOAL

Find the three-letter word which can be added to the letters in capitals to make a new word. The new word will complete the sentence sensibly.

Example: The cat sprang onto the MO.   USE

6 In our Music LES today, we played guitars.   _____
7 Look at the beautiful RAIN arching across the sky!   _____
8 Talking very loudly is called SHING.   _____
9 In the countryside you must close GS to fields behind you.   _____
10 Mrs Newman has a new PET in her sitting room.   _____

Give the missing numbers and letters in the following sequences. The alphabet has been written out to help you.

A B C D E F G H I J K L M N O P Q R S T U V W X Y Z

Example: CQ   DQ   EP   FP   GO

11   BD   FH   JL   NP   RT   _____
12   2AX   2BX   2CX   _____ 2EX   2FX
13   BAD   FEH   _____ NMP   RQT   VUX
14   abc   DEF   _____ JKL   mno   PQR
15   _____ 8EG   7IK   6MO   5QS   4UW

Time for a break! Go to Puzzle Page 42   Total

Puzzle 1

Noughts & Crosses

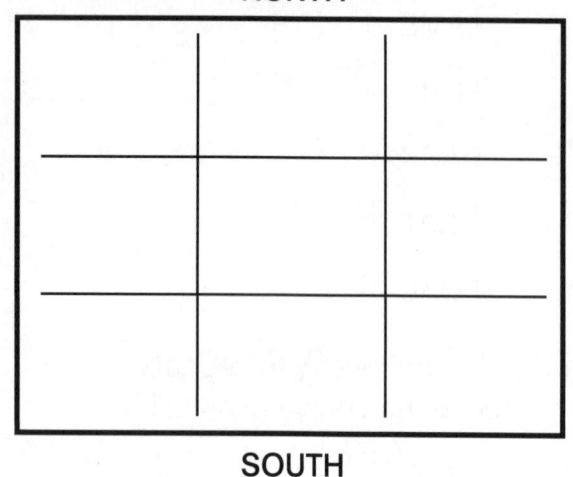

NORTH

SOUTH

Follow the instructions using the compass points, and place the Os and ✗s in the correct places. Draw a line to show who wins the game by getting three of their symbols in a row.

1   ✗ in the NW box.
2   O in the SE box.
3   ✗ in the SW box.
4   O in the W box.
5   ✗ in the NE box.
6   O in the centre.
7   ✗ in the N box.

Puzzle 2

Clock Words

Here is an unusual clock! Each of the numbers has been replaced by a letter.

Start at '12 o'clock' and go round the letters making words back up to the w at the top.

As you work your way round the clock, each missing word begins and ends with one of the letters in the squares. The missing words are shown in the body of the clock. The first one has been done for you.

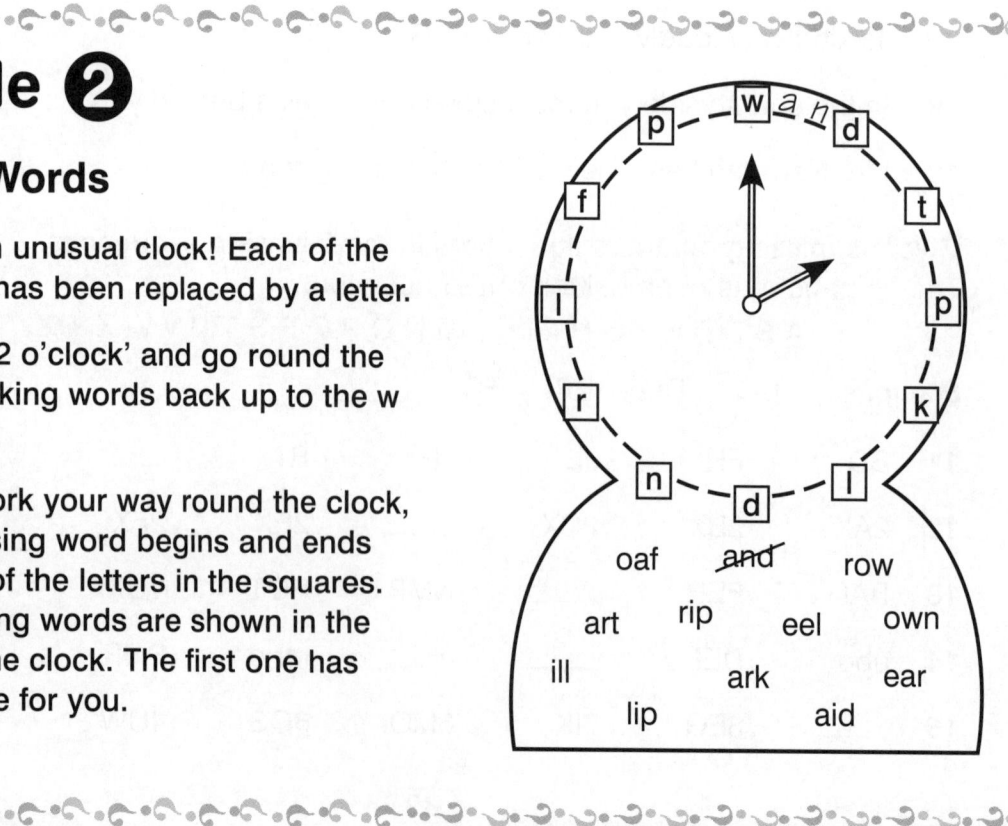

Clock letters: w a n d t p k l d n r l f p

oaf   and   row
art   rip   eel   own
ill   ark   ear
     lip   aid

Puzzle 3

Arranging Anagrams

The letters of the following words can be rearranged to make different words.

There are 3 sections to this puzzle. First try to solve the anagram by looking at Section 1. To check your answer, look at the clues in Section 2. If you still can't solve it, in Section 3 you will find the word in a mixed list.

SECTION 1

1	angel	_angle_
2	spore	_____
3	board	_____
4	teach	_____
5	reaps	_____
6	bagel	_____
7	warts	_____
8	cheap	_____
9	taste	_____
10	bleat	_____
11	throw	_____
12	least	_____

SECTION 2

1. a corner
2. cords, bonds
3. wide, not narrow
4. to swindle
5. a weapon you throw
6. the end of a building
7. animal bedding
8. a juicy fruit
9. USA is divided into 50 of these
10. you eat on it, sitting on a chair
11. value
12. not fresh

SECTION 3

~~angle~~	gable	ropes	spear
table	straw	state	peach
cheat	worth	stale	broad

Puzzle 4

Word Wall

Shade the bricks that make a word that starts with the letter in bold. Each letter in bold uses two bars. Here is an example.

B	OLD	ASH	FIN	OWN
	ARM	ALL	EAR	END

W	EAR	AIL	TOP	HIP	ASH
	BID	HEN	ALL	ARM	KIT
S	OAK	JAR	CAN	TAR	CAR
	WAN	TOW	PIT	ALL	OWL
F	ATE	ILL	AIR	ITS	OUR
	OAR	ICE	ASH	FOX	MOW
R	EEL	HOP	AIL	ATE	EAR
	OAR	ICE	ASH	SEA	MOW

Puzzle 5

Alphabet Scramble

Put the letters of each of these words into alphabetical order.

1
CHIEF	_____	SQUIRT	_____
BABY	_____	BANANA	_____
UGLY	_____	BETTER	_____
ZANY	_____	STAIR	_____

2
DANGER	_____	BADGE	_____
BABBLE	_____	PORTS	_____
SUMMER	_____	ESCAPE	_____
BACON	_____	EAGLES	_____

Now take the third letter of each of your new nonsense words and rearrange them to spell out two months of the year.

1 _____ 2 _____

Progress Grid

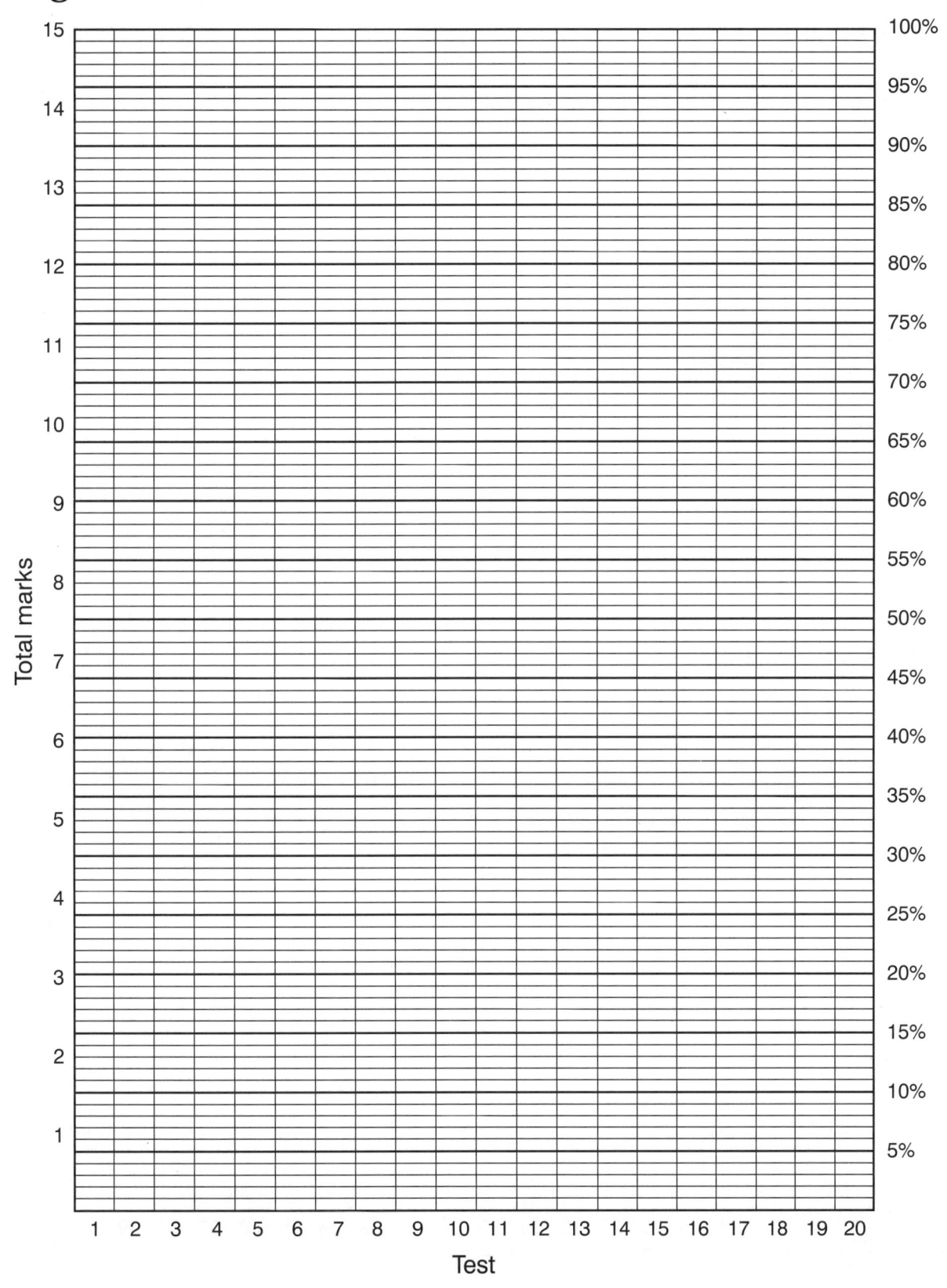

Progress Grid

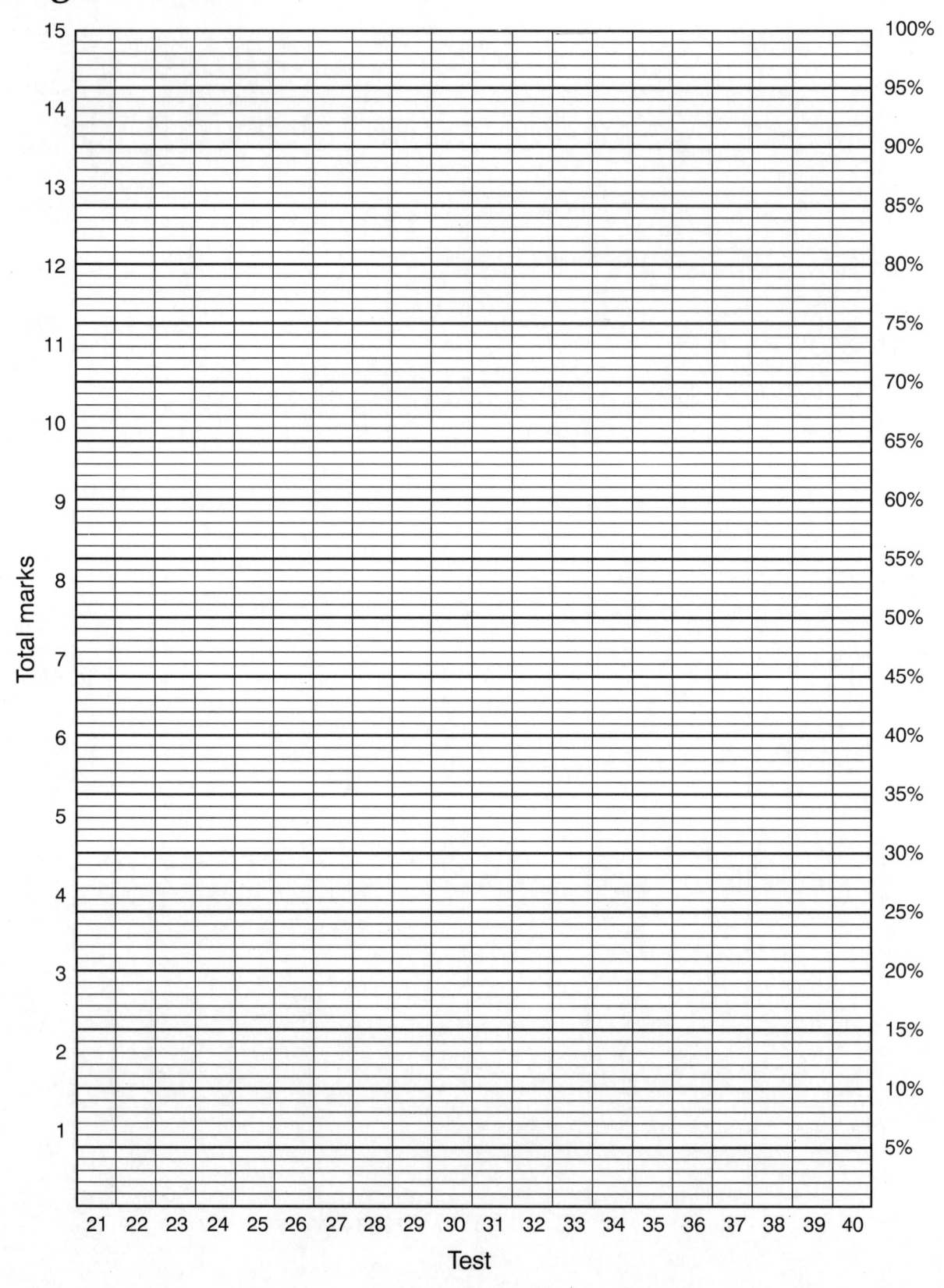